TABLE OF CONTENT

I0446852

SHOPIFY DROPSHIPPING COURSE 2023 CHEAT SHEET

Unlock Success in 2023: Your Ultimate Shopify Dropshipping Cheat Sheet

NANCY GOLD

INTRODUCTION

SHOPIFY VIP DEAL 1$ FOR 3 MONTHS

http://www.shopify.com/free-trial

FOR ALL THE BEST ECOM DEALS

https://www.kamilsattar.com/the-ecom-king-deals

BUSINESS SETUP:

Setup a LLC or LTD for tax purposes & protection (BEFORE STARTING) Make the company the name of your store, One LLC or LTD per store

Best Ecom Accountants, Osome Exclusive Tax Offer

https://stay.osome.com/ecomking12

Best Credit Cards

Capital On Tap: Use promo code: (1REFV213Z14)

https://account.capitalontap.com/apps/app ly/?promo=1REFV213Z14

Best Business Credit Card:

http://amex.co.uk/refer/mOHAmSDR8p?XL =MIANS

CHAPTER ONE

WHAT MAKES A WINNING PRODUCT IN 2023

- RECESSION PROOF & DESIGNED FOR LOWER SPENDING
- DONE FOR YOU PRODUCT - DOES THE WORK FOR YOU
- HELPS KEEP YOU ENTERTAINED FROM HOME TO SAVE MONEY
- HOME LEARNING PRODUCTS AND EDUCATIONAL
- SAVES YOU MONEY LONG TERM - AND TIME
- MULTIPURPOSE CONTENT PLATFORM TESTING

BEST DROPSHIPPING NICHES IN 2023

- FISHING - OUTDOOR SPORTS / HOBBIES
- EXTREME SPORTS - SNOWBOARDING - PADDLE BOARDING
- HOME ART - PAINTING - DRAWING - MODELING
- SPECIAL EVENTS - VALENTINES DAY - MEMORIAL EVENTS
- MOBILE GAMING - PC GAMING - ACCESSORIES
- KIDS EXTREAM TOYS / FUTRISTIC
- WOMEN FASHION - COATS - DRESSES - GYMWEAR
- HOME SELF GROOMING AND BEAUTY - MAKEUP - BEARDS

CHAPTER TWO

HOW TO FIND WINNING PRODUCTS

IN 2023

FREE METHODS

Method: 1 Viral Research
Step 1: Find a New viral products in USA / CA / UK Market

Step 2: Create an account on dropshiprabbit

Step 3: Sort By Most Impressions

Step 4: Search through all the ads and find a product that meets the criteria above by going to the AD & Website

Step 5: Once the product meets parts of the criteria above, search for the product on Ailexpress to see if its available, to find the product name see how the competitor is naming it on their website

Step 6: Once you find the product on Aliexpress, you want to see the product have 500 orders, no more than 8000 orders

Step 7: Search for the product name on the TikTok platform

Try and find the biggest pages making consistent content for the product

Step 8: read the comments and see what they could do better based on the feedback

Method: 2 Broad Niche scalping
Step 1: Go to TikTok

Step 2: These are the best niches to find products On TikTok Using This Method:

12

- Fashion
- Beauty
- Jewellery
- Kids
- Pets

Step 3: Search for keywords like:

- Summer dress - Summer Shoes
- Kid toys - Teething toy
- Dog coat - Dog bed
- Beauty tools - Makeup brush
- Earring - bracelets

Step 4: Search through all the videos, try and find the videos with the most views

Step 5: search for the broad name of the product on Aliexpress to see if its available, it doesn't have to be an exact match

Step 6: Once you find the product on Aliexpress, you want to see the product have 1000 orders

Method: 3 Brand Research
Step 1: Go to TikTok

Step 2: Search for big brand names in the niches below, for example "Pandora" "Pretty Little Thing" "Mac Makeup"

- Fashion
- Beauty
- Jewelry
- Kids
- Pets

Step 3: Look at the top vidoes and try and find a similar product on Aliexpress

Step 4: Once you find the product on Aliexpress, you want to see the product have 500 orders

Method 4: Supplier Winners

Step 1: Find viral products in USA / CA / UK Market

Step 2: Once You've found a hot product that meets the criteria find the suppliers for the product with the most orders on Aliexpress

Step 3: Message the top 3-5 suppliers the script below

Supplier Script:

Hello (SUPPLIER NAME)

My Name Is (YOURNAME) I am a Professional Droppshipper

I see you are the best supplier for (THE PRODUCT) I want to Dropship

I am wondering if you know of any other products in the (YOURNICHE) That are doing well right now for other Dropshippers

I would love to work with you on a new Dropshipping product

I look forward to hearing from you, thanks for your time

(YOUR NAME)

PAID METHODS:

Use the best tool to speed up the process of finding products peeksta.com

The best tool to find Tik Tok Winning Products

CHAPTER THREE

STORE DESIGN FOR 2023

How to Find Domain Name:

Great tool for brainstorming for those who want to find short & smart domain for the store - **Use Business Name Generator:** https://namelix.com/

In search you can indicate how long you want your domain to be, in results If the domain price that you like is very high you can try to search with small changes and you'll be surprised how great name you can generate using this strategy

Another Tool for domain search:
https://instantdomainsearch.com/

Where to create Logo & Customize Images

Create logo, Favicon, Banners, remove background & customize images in
https://canva.7eqqol.net/c/1990643/619765/10068

To use canva pro version for free for 14 days follow this link

https://canva.com

Where to create Gif's

Create Gif out of images, convert video to Gif, split & customize Gifs in

18

www.ezgif.com

Where to Create Professional Videos

Create gold-standard videos like a Pro

sign-up using the link https://invideo.io

Join the InVideo community to get feedback on your videos and learn from 20K+ other marketers and creators who are on it: https://bit.ly/36Bxf5P

Follow InVideo's official YouTube channel for more hacks on creating videos with ease - InVideo Official: https://www.youtube.com/channel/UCgxM iiBKk-xYskc2KNLiBTg

What Platform to Use:

💻 🔔 Shopify 90 Days For $1 VIP OFFER ENDS SOON ☞

http://www.shopify.com/free-trial

Claim your free domain name:

https://www.hostinger.com/recommended/ecomking?ignore_geo

Recommended Chrome Extensions

Colorzilla Chrome Extension - To identify color codes:

https://chrome.google.com/webstore/detail/colorzilla

AliSave – Download AliExpress Images & Videos:

https://chrome.google.com/webstore/detail/alisave-download-aliexpre/nbhfcmbdimdbbclfngkjfmgmjhnkjocl?hl=en

Tool for Keyword research – Chrome extension Keywords Everywhere:

https://chrome.google.com/webstore/detail/keywords-everywhere-keywo/hbapdpeemoojbophdfndmlgdhppljgmp/RK%3D2/RS%3Ded0KEDJEEUOOa1yG0dfw.62hzeE-

Extra Support for Content

Content writing:

https://www.conversion.ai/pricing

Check your texts for plagiarism using - Plagiarism Detector:

https://plagiarismdetector.net/

TOP APPS 2023

APPS YOU NEED TO INSTALL:

- AutoDS
- Loox
- Klaviyo
- SMS Bump
- Tidio
- Bundle Bear
- BeProfit

CHAPTER FOUR

Klaviyo Setup:

Welcome Series 1

Form From: Anna @ Just Decore

Newsletter Welcome Subject: Welcome to the Just Decore Community

Title: The Exclusive Home Decor Collection

Dear valued customer,

Welcome to Just Decore! We are thrilled to have you as a part of our community and look forward to providing you with the highest quality home decor items and excellent customer service.

As a token of our appreciation, we would like to offer you a special discount code for your first purchase with us. Simply use the code SAVE5 at checkout to receive $5 off your order.

In the coming days, you will receive a series of emails introducing you to our store and the various products and services we offer. We hope these emails will help you get to know us better and find the products that are right for you.

If you have any questions or concerns, please don't hesitate to reach out to us. Our customer service team is always happy to help.

Thank you again for choosing our store. We can't wait to serve you and become your go-to destination for all your shopping needs.

Sincerely,

Anna Just Decore

2

In the next email of the welcome series, you can introduce your customers to your store's best-selling products and highlight any special deals or promotions you have available. You can also include customer reviews or testimonials to give potential customers an idea of the quality of your products and service.

Additionally, you can share more about your company's mission and values, and how your products align with those values. This can help customers feel more connected to your brand and understand what sets you apart from other stores.

For example:

Dear valued customer,

Thank you for joining our community! We hope you enjoyed your first experience with us and are looking forward to providing you with many more.

As promised, we wanted to introduce you to some of our best-selling products. [Insert product descriptions and images here]. These products have consistently received high ratings and rave reviews from our customers, and we are confident they will become some of your favourites as well.

We also wanted to let you know about a special promotion we are currently running. [Insert promotion details here]. Be sure to take advantage of this limited-time offer while you can!

At [Your Store], we are committed to providing high-quality products that align with our values of sustainability, social responsibility, and innovation. We believe that by offering products that align with these values, we can make a positive impact on the world and our customers' lives.

Thank you again for choosing our store. We are always here to assist with any questions or concerns you may have.

Sincerely,

[Your Name]

[Your Store]

3

In the next email of the welcome series, you can focus on building a relationship with your customers and encouraging them to engage with your store. This could include inviting them to sign up for your email list or newsletter to receive updates about new products, sales, and special offers.

You can also encourage customers to follow your social media accounts or join your loyalty program to stay connected and earn rewards.

Additionally, you can highlight any resources or services that you offer to help customers make informed purchasing decisions, such as product guides, size charts, or a customer service hotline.

Here is an example of what the next email in the welcome series could look like:

Dear valued customer,

We hope you are enjoying your experience with our store so far! As a part of our community, we want to make sure you are fully informed about all the resources and services we offer to help you make the most of your shopping experience.

We are active on social media and would love for you to follow us on [insert social media platforms] to stay connected and get a behind-the-scenes look at our company and products.

Finally, if you have any questions or need help making a purchase, our customer service team is always here to assist. You can reach us by email or live chat on our website. We also have a number of product guides and size charts available to help you find the perfect fit.

Thank you again for choosing our store. We value your business and are committed to providing the best shopping experience possible.

Sincerely,

[Your Name]

[Your Store]

Abandoned Cart Emails

Template 1:

Subject: Don't miss out on [product name]!

Hi {{ first_name|default:"" }},

We noticed that you left [product name] in your cart on our website. We hope everything is okay and that you're still interested in making a purchase.

To make it easier for you, we've included a direct link to your cart below. All you have to do is click the link and complete the checkout process.

{{ event.extra.checkout_url }}

If you have any questions or need assistance, don't hesitate to reach out to us. We're here to help.

Thanks for considering [product name] and we hope to see you back on our site soon!

Best regards,

[Your name]

[Your Store]

Template 2:

Subject: [Product name] is waiting for you!

Hi {{ first_name|default:"" }},

We hope you're doing well! We noticed that you left [product name] in your cart on our website and we wanted to remind you about it.

We think you'll love [product name] and we're here to help make your purchase as easy as possible. If you have any questions or need assistance, just let us know.

To make it even easier for you, we're offering a special discount on [product name] just for you. Use code [discount code] at checkout to receive [discount amount] off your purchase.

Don't miss out on this opportunity to get [product name] at a discounted price. Click the link below to complete your purchase.

{{ event.extra.checkout_url }}

We hope to see you back on our site soon!

Best regards,

[Your name]

[Your Store]

Template 3:

Subject: Your cart is still waiting for you – and so is our [discount or promotion]!

Hi {{ first_name|default:"" }},

We hope this email finds you well. We noticed that you left some items in your cart on our site and wanted to remind you that they're still waiting for you.

To make it even more tempting to complete your purchase, we're currently offering a [discount or promotion] on all orders. This is a great opportunity to save on your purchase.

To take advantage of this offer and complete your purchase, just click on the link below:

{{ event.extra.checkout_url }}

If you have any questions or need help with your order, don't hesitate to contact us. We're here to help make your shopping experience as smooth as possible.

Thanks for choosing [store name]!

Best regards,

[Your name]

[Your Store]

I hope these templates are helpful! Let me know if you have any questions.

Customer Thank You

Subject: Your [store name] Order Confirmation

Hi {{ first_name|default:"" }},

Thank you for your order from [store name]! We're excited to get your products on their way to you.

Your order will be shipped within [time frame] and you'll receive a shipment notification email with tracking information once it's on its way.

If you have any questions or need help with your order, don't hesitate to contact us. We're here to help make your shopping experience as smooth as possible.

Thanks again for choosing [store name]!

Best regards,

[Your name]

CHAPTER FIVE

Tidio AI Responder Message:

We try our best to ship items as fast as we can. Please allow 4-7 days production time for your order to ship out. Average shipping times are 15-21 days. Tracking numbers will be updated 3-5 days after your order has been SHIPPED. If you haven't received a tracking number after 7 days, please email us at company@email.com.

SMS Bump Full Setup:

<u>SETUP SECTION</u>

1.   Go to View Guide in Welcome Section of Dashboard and set up your compliance.

2. Enable Marketing Checkbox and ensure it is not preselected as this is against regulations.

3. Go back to your Store>Settings>Checkout>Email marketing and make sure the preselect option is disabled.

4. Scroll down to Checkout Language and select Manage Check Out.

5. Go back to SMS Bump and copy (CMD + C / Control +C) the language provided below:

a. { Sign up for exclusive offers and news via text messages and/or email }

6. Go back to store and select Settings>Checkout>Check out language and select manage check out language.

7. Click Control F to search for phrase and type in Accept Marketing\ Checkbox Label at top of page in search bar.

8. Paste the text from line 5 into the Accept marketing Checkbox section and Save Settings.

9. Go to your cart and it should look like below.

10. Go to Shipping address phone number and make it Optional or Required.

11. Go back to Shopify Store, select Form Options> Shipping Address Phone Numbers and select optional or required and save your settings.

12. Go back to SMSBump Instructions. Copy and Paste text on store

13. Go back to store>Manage Languages and search at top for Phone label.

14. Paste the information provided by SMSBump into the field.

a.   { Phone number and email for exclusive offers. }

15. Your page should look like below. This is where you customers will share their phone number for texts.

16. Next go to Privacy Policy. You can go back to your SMSBump instructions and copy and paste the necessary language to put on your store.

17. Go back to Shopify Store>Settings>Legal>Privacy Policy

18. Paste provide text into the field as instructed and Save Settings.

a.　{ Text Marketing and Notifications:　By subscribing to text notifications you agree to receive recurring automated marketing messages at the phone number provided. Consent is not a condition of purchase. Reply STOP to unsubscribe. HELP for help. Msg & Data rates may apply. For more info view our Terms of Service.}

19. Check out Footer Language

20. Go to theme settings>actions and select Edit Languages.

21. Select Checkout and Systems and search for phrase Checkout Shop Policy.

22. Paste the data in the field and Save Settings

a.　{I consent to receive recurring automated marketing by text message through an automated text dialing system.

Consent is not a condition to purchase. STOP to cancel, HELP for help. Message & Data rates may apply. View Privacy Policy.}

23. Below is what you should see on your store

24. Enable Quiet Hours. Important!

25. Set up Complete. Enjoy!

AUTOMATIONS SETUP

SMS - Abandoned Cart
1 (Send after 15min)

Hey {FirstName}, it looks like you left something in your cart. Don't miss out on the [product name] - it's going fast! Click here to finish your purchase: {AbandonedCheckoutUrl}. If you have any questions or need help, just reply to this message and we'll be happy to assist.

2 (Send after 2 Hours) - Add a 10% Discount

Hi {FirstName}, we noticed that you left some items in your cart and we don't want you to miss out on any of them! Click here to complete your purchase and get [product name] and with a 10% Discount using the Code „{DiscountCode}": {AbandonedCheckoutUrl}. If you have any

43

questions, just reply to this message and we'll be happy to help.

3 (Send after 20 Hours) - Add a 20% Discount

Hey {FirstName}, it looks like you left a few items in your cart. Don't miss out on the [product name] - it's going fast! Click here to finish your purchase with a 20% Discount using the Code „{DiscountCode}": {AbandonedCheckoutUrl} . If you have any questions or need help, just reply to this message and we'll be happy to assist.

SMS - Product Upsell Sequence

1 (Send after 1 Hour)

Hey {FirstName}, thanks for your recent purchase of [product name]! We hope you're enjoying it. We noticed that you might also be interested in

{RecommendProductName}. It's a great complement to [product name] and we think you'll love it. Click here to check it out: {RecommendProductUrl}. If you have any questions, just reply to this message and we'll be happy to help.

2 (Send after 12 Hours)

Hi {FirstName}, just wanted to remind you about the great deal we're currently offering on {RecommendProductName. It's a perfect complement to your [product name] and we think you'll love it. Plus, use code {DiscountCode} at checkout to save an extra [discount amount] on your purchase. Click here to check it out: {RecommendProductUrl}. If you have any questions, just reply to this message and we'll be happy to help.

SMS - Customer Win back Sequence

1 (Send after 30 Days)

Hey {BillingFirstName}, we noticed that it's been a while since you made a purchase from our store. We miss you! To show you how much we value you, we're offering a special deal just for you - use code {DiscountCode} at checkout to save [discount amount] on your next purchase. Click here to check out what's new: {SiteUrl}. We hope to see you back soon!

2 (Send after 10 Days)

Hi {BillingFirstName}, we hope you're doing well. We just wanted to remind you about the special deal we're offering to bring you back to our store - use code {DiscountCode} at checkout to save [discount amount] on your next purchase. We've got some new arrivals that we think you'll love. Click here to check them out: [link to store]. We hope to see you back soon!

CHAPTER SIX

Website Pages

Privacy Policy

(YOUR BRAND NAME HERE) is compliant with The General Data Protection Regulation (GDPR) (EU) 2016/679.

It means that we are open about our methods of tracking and use of the visitors' personal data, and you can freely check what exactly we're doing to it.

At www.yourbusinessemail, we collect:

- Your name and surname
- Your email address
- Your physical address
- Your phone number
- The data about the browser and device you use to view the store
- The way you navigate the store

We gather your contact details because they are necessary to accept and process your orders, and to make sure you've got your packages.

We gather the details of your technical equipment and on-site behavior in order to make our store more user-friendly, and to personalize our store services for you (for example, to automatically switch the store to the mobile version.)

Our store works with outer companies that help us provide the best service for you, and these third parties also use some of the personal details you're leaving. We limit the data they can access to only what is necessary for them to perform their obligations.

- Payment services use your credit card number, your name and surname to verify and process your payments for our products
- Our manufacturers and stock keepers use the data of your order contents to assemble the necessary package for you
- Postal services use your first name, last name, and physical address to arrange the product delivery for you

- Mass mailing services use your email address to send you emails (if you have subscribed for them)

If you keep browsing our webstore after reading this Privacy Policy, you give us the consent to use your personal details for the purposes explained above.

- If you don't agree to these terms, please leave the website.
- You can email us at supportyourbusinessemail.com and ask:
- To receive the copy of your personal details we have collected
- To delete your personal details from our system
- To withdraw your consent (if you previously agreed to provide us with the data, but then changed your mind)

We are doing our best to guarantee the security of your personal details while keeping and using them.

Thank you for your cooperation!

Returns & Refunds

Order cancellation

All orders can be cancelled until they are shipped. If your order has been paid and you need to change or cancel it, you must contact us within 12 hours. Once the packaging and shipping process has started, it can no longer be cancelled.

Refunds

We offer a 100% money back guarantee on all products that are defective or damaged during shipping. Just let us know and we will provide a return address and a replacement or refund as preferred.

If you are unsatisfied with your order – please contact our support and we will do our best to help you out!

Customers will be responsible for paying return shipping costs.

We do not issue the refund if:

your order does not arrive due to factors within your control (e.g. providing the wrong shipping address)

*You can submit refund requests within 15 days after the guaranteed period for delivery (45 days) has expired. You can do it by sending a message on Contact Us page.

Terms Of Service

We provide services to you subject to the notices, terms, and conditions set forth in this agreement. Besides, you will obey the rules, guidelines, policies, terms, and conditions applicable to such services before you use them. We reserve the right to change this site and these terms and conditions at any time.

Before proceeding, please read this agreement because accessing, browsing, or otherwise using the Site indicates your agreement to all the terms and conditions in this agreement.

You shall not upload, distribute, or otherwise publish through this Site any Content, information, or other material that (a) includes any bugs, viruses, worms, trap doors, Trojan horses, or other harmful code or properties; (b) is libelous, threatening, defamatory, obscene, indecent, pornographic, discriminatory, or could give rise to any civil or criminal liability under the laws of the U.S. or the laws of any other country that may apply; or (c)violates or infringes upon the copyrights, patents, trademarks, service marks, trade secrets, or other proprietary rights of any person. www.yourbusinessdomain may give you an account identification and password to enable you to access and use certain portions of this Site. Each time you use a password or identification, you are deemed to be authorized to access and use the Site in a manner consistent with the terms and conditions of this agreement, and

www.yourbusinessdomain has no obligation to investigate the source of any such access or use of the Site.

By accepting these Terms of Use through your use of the Site, you certify that you are 18 years of age or older. If you are under 18 years old please use this Site only under the supervision of a parent or legal guardian. Subject to the terms and conditions of this agreement, hereby grants you a limited, revocable, non-transferable, and non-exclusive license to access and use the Site by displaying it on your Internet browser only for the purpose of shopping and not for any commercial use or use on behalf of any third party, except as explicitly permitted by

www.yourbusinessdomain in advance. Any violation of this Agreement shall result in the immediate revocation of the license granted in this paragraph without notice to you.

Unless explicitly permitted by our company in advance, all materials, including images, text, illustrations, designs, icons, photographs, programs, music clips or downloads, video clips and written and other materials that are part of this Site (collectively, the "Contents") are intended solely for personal, non-commercial use. You may not make any commercial use of any of the information provided on the Site or make any use of the Site for the benefit of another business. We reserve the right to refuse service, terminate accounts, and/or cancel orders in its discretion, including, without limitation, if we believe that customer conduct violates applicable laws or is harmful to our interests. You may not reproduce, distribute, display, sell, lease, transmit, create derivative works from, translate, modify, reverse-engineer, disassemble, decompile, or otherwise exploit this Site or any portion of it unless expressly permitted by our company in writing.

You will be solely responsible for all access to and use of this site by anyone using the password and identification originally assigned to you whether or not such access to and use of this site is actually authorized by you, including without limitation, all communications and transmissions and all obligations (including without limitation financial obligations) incurred through such access or use. You are solely responsible for protecting the security and confidentiality of the password and identification assigned to you. You shall immediately notify

www.yourbusinessdomain of any unauthorized use of your password or identification or any other breach or threatened breach of this Site's security.

Shipping & Delivery

FREE SHIPPING

We are glad to bring our customers great value and service. That's why we provide free shipping from our warehouses in Europe & USA by FEDEX, USPS, DHL, DPD.

SHIPPING TO OVER 200 COUNTRIES

We are proud to offer international shipping services. However, there are some locations we are unable to ship to. If you happen to be from one of those countries we will contact you.

LOST/MISSING PACKAGES

(YOUR BRAND NAME HERE) are not liable if the incorrect address is placed during the checkout process. Please make sure that your billing and shipping address is correct before processing your order. If we have made an error we will fully take responsibility for the original order that was made for you at no charge.

CUSTOMS

We are not responsible for any custom fees once the items have shipped. By purchasing our products, you consent that one or more packages may be shipped to you and may get custom fees when they arrive in your country.

SHIPPING TIME

Shipping time varies by location. These are our estimates:

Location Shipping Time	Estimated
United States	3-5 Business days
Canada, Europe	6-10 Business days
Australia, New Zealand	12-14 Business days
Central & South America	8-14 Business days
Asia	8-12 Business days
Africa	8-14 Business days

Max delivery time – 20 business days.

*This doesn't include our 1-3 day processing time.

*All shipping times exclude clearance/customs delays

TRACKING INFORMATION

You will receive an email with a tracking number once your order is shipped but sometimes due to free shipping tracking is not available.

MY TRACKING SAYS "NO INFORMATION AVAILABLE AT THE MOMENT".

For some shipping companies, it takes 1-5 business days for the tracking information to update on the system. If your order was placed more than 5 business days ago and there is still no information on your tracking number, please contact us.

WILL MY ITEMS BE SENT IN ONE PACKAGE?

For logistical reasons, items in the same purchase will sometimes be sent in separate packages, even if you've specified combined shipping.

If you have any other questions, please contact us and we will do our best to help you out.

Our Story

(**YOURSTORENAME**). is one of the world's leading online fashion brands that specialise in (YOURNICHE). We are a fast growing fashion company because we always put the customer first. A customer cantered shopping experience has always been our main goal, and we pride ourselves in our comprehensive policies that have put us in a realm above and beyond in the industry of fashion. Here at **(YOURSTORENAME).**we believe in passing along deeply thoughtful fashion designs to our customers so they can make a bold fashion statement

Our company is built on three core principles:

- Excellent designs
- Unique 1 off designs
- Excellent customer service

We believe that serving our customers upholds a responsibility to ensure that they are satisfied with their purchases. We will do our best to make sure that our customers are happy. We believe we can create a good impact in the fashion industry forever by focusing on our customers' thoughts.

We're glad you've found your way to our online fashion store We hope you'll be back often and spread the word to all your friends! Shop with us today and see the(**YOURSTORENAME**).difference.

FAQs

1. What comes in the DIGITAL Pack?

You will get the following:

- High-quality Unique lightroom presets
- 5 presets
- Lifetime access to all updates and new icons

2. How do I receive the digital Pack?

After purchase, you will receive a dropbox link in your email order confirmation which will enable you to download the digital pack

3. How do I add the presets to my images

For step-by-step instructions please <u>click here</u>

4. How do I receive updates & new icons?

When we add presets or make any updates, this will be added to the Dropbox folder which you will have access to

You will also receive an email about any updates so you will always be kept in the loop

5. How do I get in contact with you?

Please contact us at the following email address:

Alternatively, please feel free to drop us a message on instagram

What Content You Need For Advertising

Use Billo for custom content:

https://billo.app/

Use Invideo to edit your videos:

sign-up using the link https://invideo.io/

UGC Videos 3-5 Per Product - The More The Better

- High Quality Images 3-5 Per Product
- 1-2 Testimonial Videos
- 10 Ad Copies Per Product - Short - Medium - Long
- 10 Ad Headlines Per Product

CHAPTER SEVEN

GOOGLE ADS TUTORIAL

(SEARCH ADS + SHOPPING ADS +

PERFORMANCE MAX)

by Jorge Vieira

Pre-launch checklist (detailed walkthrough in the video)

Get Keywords Everywhere and purchase some credits:
https://keywordseverywhere.com/

- Create Google Ads Account
- Create Google Analytics Account and integrate with Shopify
- Create Merchant Center Account
- Setup Google Sales Channel on Shopify

- Setup Shipping Settings on Shopify (I recommend Free Shipping)

A few extra pre-start recommendations:

#1 - Use keywords everywhere and research some keywords for your search campaign. I would recommend anything above 1 000 searches/month and under 20 000

searches/month. Other search volumes are okay too but do watch the video tutorial carefully so that you don't make the mistake of spending all your budget very quickly on a search term with a very high search volume.

#2 - Do some SEO optimization for your product titles and descriptions. This will increase your Google Relevance Score and help you rank higher.

Recommendation: Start by including your search terms with the highest monthly search volume in your product titles, by descending order of volume. If your highest volume term is "rotating phone holder" and your second highest volume term is "phone tripod" your SEO title in Shopify should be "Rotating phone holder phone tripod (and so on)". This does make your title look weird but remember that we're doing this in the Shopify setting for SEO title and SEO description, not the main title and main description, also as explained in the video.

You can include 3-4 or more search terms in your title and as many as you can find in your description. Sometimes even seemingly unrelated terms in your description will trigger profitable search terms!

Testing and Scaling (Search Ads)

- Run through your initial keywords campaign and turn off anything that spends your break-even point without making a sale.
- Keep cycling new keywords.
- Monitor your search terms. Exclude search terms leaking money and add profitable search terms as new keywords in a new ad group.
- Keep testing and increase the budget on your most profitable keywords, according to ROAS. Keep in mind that you'll reach a plateau after which it will be hard to increase your budget even further, since there is a limit on the monthly search volume for each keyword.
- Testing and Scaling (Shopping Ads)

- Wait for your ads to start spending and give them at least 7 days of spend before making any changes. Remember, shopping ads take longer to optimize!
- Turn off anything that spends your break-even point without making a sale.
- Only make changes once a week!
- After the first week of spending (the initial days when your ads barely spend anything don't count!) increase your bid by 20% on anything that is profitable and decrease your bid by 20% on anything that is unprofitable in the last 7 days.
- Keep monitoring search terms, you want to exclude unprofitable search terms that may be leaking money.

Performance Max

Performance Max is my recommendation for beginners starting Google Ads in 2023.

Assets:

To start a Performance Max campaign I recommend that you get the following assets (minimum):

- 3 different sizes logos of your company
- 5 video ads with different formats (mix of vertical and square aspect ratios)
- 15 picture ads with different formats (mix of vertica and square aspect ratios)

Campaign setup:

If you're starting with a fresh Google Ads account with no data, I'd recommend you start by optimising for Conversions as opposed to conversion value.

When setting up your ads, fill in with at least 5 headlines, 5 long headlines and 5 descriptions. When doing so, try to use as many relevant keywords to your target audience as possible as this will be an important point of intelligence for the machine learning system that guides delivery in a Performance Max campaign.

Make sure to set up an audience signal with as many relevant data points to your target audience as possible, such as: demographics, search interest and general interests.

When doing targeting for a new offer I'd recommend that you start by keeping your target as narrow as possible: start with the best possible pocket of your audience and then expand once you have data, as this will help Google's machine learning system to optimise based on the data that you gather from existing conversions.

Once you start running your Performance Max campaign, remember to let it run for at least a week before making changes. Performance Max is heavily based on machine learning and making changes too early will compromise the learning phase.

Questions?
Instagram:
https://www.instagram.com/jorgemoitaviei ra/

YouTube:
https://www.youtube.com/c/JorgeVieiraEc
om

Facebook:
https://www.facebook.com/profile.php?id=
100012155713751

CHAPTER EIGHT

YOUTUBE ADS TUTORIAL

by Vedank Mohan

Before starting

- Targeting options recap:
- Very similar to Facebook
- You can target specific YouTube channels and videos
- You can target specific keywords
- You can create audiences based on the search intent
- You can use audiences targeting (in market, life events, affinity, remarketing)

Campaign Structure

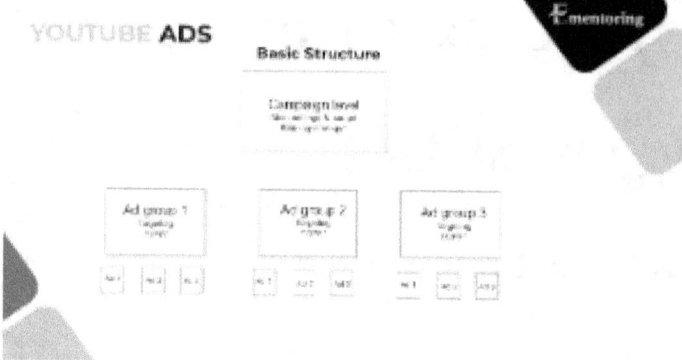

Audience Testing Structure

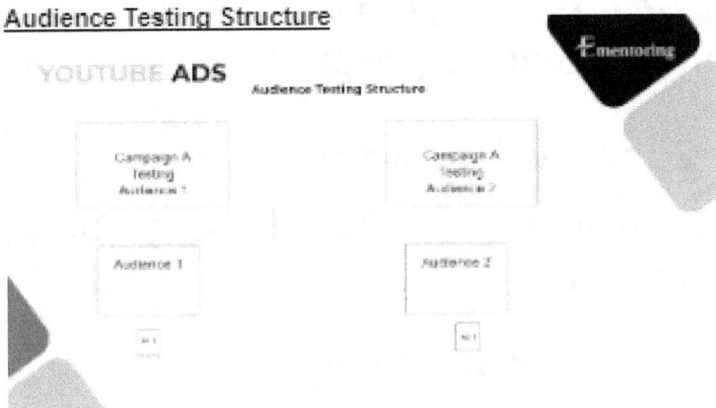

Creative Testing Structure

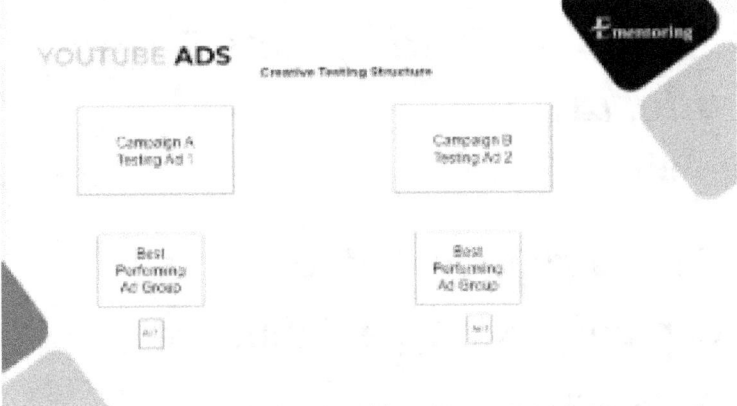

Bidding Strategies

Automatic Bidding / Maximise conversions

- Google will deliver as many conversions as possible based on your budget
- Good to warming up your account

Target Cost per Action (TCPA)

- Google will do his best to deliver conversions accordingly your TCPA
- If TCPA is too low, budget will not be spent
- Prefered method

Campaign 1: Product and brand consideration

Campaign

- Campaign type: Video
- Campaign Subtype: Influence consideration

- Click "Continue"
- Campaign daily budget should be $5/day for first week, after the week optimize campaign and increase budget upto $20
- Choose location and language

Ad group

- Define demographic
- Define audience segments
- You can define keywords and placements as well in another ad group
- Maximum bidding should be 0.10 - 0.15(Increase bidding if it doesn't work)

Ad

- Video ad format skippable in-stream ad and In-feed video

- We suggests skippable in-stream ad and try to add a call-to-action and headline in it

Campaign 2: <u>Sales Campaign</u>

- Keep only add to basket, begin checkout and purchases as goals in the campaign
- Click "Continue"
- Bid Strategy TCPA
- Add daily budget
- Select locations and languages
- Add extensions - Sitelink extension

Ad group

- Define demographic
- Define audience segments

- You can define keywords and placements as well in another ad group
- You can target specific channels or videos

Ad

- Video ad format skippable in-stream ad and In-feed video
- We suggests skippable in-stream ad and try to add a call-to-action and headline in it.

Suppliers & Logistics

<u>Dropshipping Suppliers</u>

- CJ Dropshipping
- My Favourite
- Wiio

- Yakyoffy
- HyperSKU
- AliBaba Dropshipping
- uDroppy
- Zendrop

Bulk-Ordering Suppliers

- AliBaba

Common Questions When Bulk Ordering

What are the benefits of ordering in bulk?

- Increased product quality
- Decrease COGS
- More control of supply chain
- Decreased shipping times
- Can create custom bundles/offers

What are the downsides of ordering in bulk?

- Risk

When do I order in bulk?

- 2-4 weeks of consistent sales
- Depends on your risk tolerance as well

How much do I order in bulk?

- Depends on risk tolerance and current volume
- Project how much stock you'll need for around 3 weeks and go from there
- Start with a small order in case your store dies out
- As your brand grows and become more confident, make bigger orders

Fulfilling Orders When Bulk Ordering

- There's 3 different methods of fulfilment that I've used when bulk ordering

<u>3PL (in China)</u>

- Takes care of IOSS for you
- Great communication
- More expensive than usual
- I used Ecommops

<u>Private Agent Warehouse (pre much a smaller 3PL in China)</u>

- Great communication
- A bit cheaper
- Can't take care of IOSS

<u>In-house fulfillment (fulfilling from my location)</u>

- Full control of the supply chain
- Faster shipping (3-5 days to USA)
- Easier to create different bundles/offers

- Doesn't take that much time, a lot cheaper than a 3PL in USA

CHAPTER NINE

Facebook ads Tutorial

By Suraj Singh

- Columns
- Budget
- Results
- Cost per result
- Amount spent
- Purchase roas
- Unique link clicks
- Cost per unique link clicks
- Outbound CTR (unique)
- Impressions
- CPM

- Frequency
- Video Avg Play Time
- Content views
- Add to cart
- Initiate checkout
- Purchase
- Cost per add to cart
- Cost per checkout
- Cost per purchase
- Video plays at 75%
- Video plays at 95%

Initial Testing Structure and Budget

In this section, we will cover how you can test products efficiently without overspending.

Structure of testing campaign

1 ABO CAMPAIGN

→   6-10 ADSETS (Single Interest targeting) - $10-15/day

→ 3 - 5 different creatives in each adset

Budget Guidelines for adsets

- To be budget efficient, you can start with atleast $10/day for each adset and let it spend for 3 days or your breakeven cost per purchase (BECPP). If your product is mid high or ticket item ($90+ selling price), you can also start with $15/day for each adset.

Targeting Setup (Adset level)

- Single Interest Targeting - When your pixel is new or you are trying a totally new product, your pixel doesn't know your exact audience. In such cases, you need to provide your potential buying audience to facebook to gather better data. Single interest works best in such cases.Try to find interests in your niche that are broad (at least 5M+). The bigger the size is, the better. For an example, if you're testing a pet product: Test the interest - i love dogs. Essentially, all your adsets would have different interests each.

You can use these tools to find niche specific interests - https://peeksta.com/

- Select your pixel and select conversion event - Purchase
- Locations - you can select Epacket or T5 (US, UK, CAN, AU, NZ)
- Start date and time - 12am (as per your ad account timezone) for the next day.
- Age - normally 21 and above.
- Select Automatic Placement

Ad Creative Set Up

Essentially you would have 3-5 ad creative variations that you'll duplicate across each ad set.

Naming: AD1

Select create an ad

Single image or a video

AD copy: make sure you explain the main benefits of the product in a fun and engaging way (imagine telling a friend about this great product) and always add a call to action with your offer at the end

Headline: product name

Description: Offer Ends in 48 hours

Call to action: shop now

Website Link: product page

90

At the ad level, add UTM params

Here's the text you need :

utm_source=Facebook&utm_medium=cpc &utm_campaign={{campaign.name}}&utm_ content={{ad.name}}&utm_term={{adset.na me}}

What are your next steps after launching your ads? (Optimization)

We follow a very strict rule to ensure we are spending the right amount. Essentially, we want to find winners and not waste too much money and time forcing something to work. Here is what to look out for:

After Day 1 -

Go to the ad level - Cut down ads that has spent over $8 and giving terrible CPC (>$3 or $1 above your average CPC)

Further Optimization after BE-CPP spent

- Let each adset spend atleast BE-CPP (usually for 2-3 days)

- After an adset spent BECPP

    - Did it make any sales?

        :Yes → Let it run for another BECPP spend.

        : No → if shown good CPC(< $1) and good CTR (> 2%), let it run for another day.

        → If bad CPC,CTR, no ATC → Kill

        → If after a day, still no sales → Kill

- After spending another BE-CPP

- Is the ROAS above your BE-ROAS?

: Yes → let it run.

: No → Kill

- If no Adset (after testing atleast 10-15 interests) bring any sale → Switch to next product

- Once you find 2-3 profitable adsets, your first goal is to find similar winning audiences by using different interests related to these interests. You can use suggestions from facebook to find similar interests.

- If any of the running adset brings 4+ sales profitably → Scale it.

Scaling

1- after killing the bad adsets you want to duplicate the best performers 3 - 5 times and test new interest that are similar to the ones which performed the best you can use the suggestions tab on the adset level

2- scaling with CBOs after an adset hits 4 - 5 sales with a profitable roas you want to duplicate it 5 times into a CBO campaign with a 10x budget meaning if you were doing 10$ in the testing campaign the scaling campaign should be 100$

Use this tool to calculate your breakeven ROAS: https://thedropshiptoolkit.com/

NOTE: when scaling you should always use an existing post on the ad level to collect social proof

Optimization:

If yesterday ROAS >~ your desired ROAS (Ex: BE ROAS + 20% margin); scale budget 20% (vertical scaling). / Duplicate adset 2-3x at higher budgets. You can also duplicate the campaign at a higher budget.

If yesterday ROAS ~ BE ROAS; no action needed

If last 3 days + today ROAS ~ BE ROAS; reduce budget 20% (stabilize).

If last 3 days + today ROAS < BE ROAS; turn off the ad sets (kill losers).

Whenever you see a campaign is unprofitable, always check at the adset and ad level. There may be a case where a certain audience or creative is ruining the overall performance of the campaign. So, kill the bad adset or creative.

Retargeting campaign

: Always have 10-15% of your total budget allocated to retargeting. They are your warm customers and can be converted easily.

Structure for retargeting

1 ABO CAMPAIGN - You can also try a CBO campaign if that works for you.

Adsets - Try MOF (middle of the funnel) and BOF(bottom of the funnel) audiences.

Like

- 1 adset of - 75% Video views + 95% video views

- 1 adset of - Website visitors

- 1 adset of - FB/IG Engagements

exclude BOF audiences if you are testing MOF audiences. Most imp is to remove buyers from it.

Unless you are retargeting buyers with new products or special offers, you should exclude buyers from each retargeting adsets.

Budget

You can run retargeting adset at low budgets like $10-$15/day per adset.

Retargeting audiences and LLA's that works currently:

Low level engagement (easy to capture on fresh Pixels/ad accounts):

VV 50-95%

All website visitors 30 days

FB/IG Engagement

High level engagement (Shopify/Klaviyo data - need more historic data):

People who ATC

All email subscribers.

Buyers (great for LLA's)

CHAPTER TEN

TikTok Ads

- Metrics
- Status
- Budget
- Bid (ad group level)
- Ad Scheduling (ad group level)
- Ad Group Name (ad level)
- Total Cost
- CPC
- CPM
- CTR
- Impressions
- Clicks
- Total Add to Cart
- Total Initiate Checkout
- Total Complete Payment

- Cost per Complete Payment
- CVR
- Cost per Add to Cart
- Cost per Initiate Checkout

Testing Strategy

Campaign Level

- Conversion Campaign
- Naming: [product name] Testing Campaign [Date]

Ad Group Level

- Naming: [audience]-1
- # of Ad Groups will depend on your budget
  - If you have a smaller budget, use 3 open ad groups to test
  - If you have a larger budget, use 3 open + 3 interest based ad groups

Placement

- TikTok ONLY
- Turn OFF user comments
- Turn OFF Video Downloads

Creative Type

- Keep Automated Creative Optimization OFF

Targeting

- Audience - leave it empty if broad, select any broad interest that makes sense for your niche for interest targeting
- Demo: USA & Canada (or whatever other country you want to targete)

- I found that if I'm selling in both USA & Canada, having both in the ad group works better
- Gender - No Limit (unless it's obviously for a male or female)
- Age - 18+
- Languages - No Limit
- None for 3 ad groups
- Pick interests that make sense for the other 3
- Targeting Expansion - leave it OFF

Budget & Schedule

- Daily Budget - $20
- Schedule - next day at 12am (00:00)
- Don't touch anything else
- **Bidding & Optimization**
  - Optimization Goal – Conversion
  - Bid Strategy - Lowest Cost

Ad Level

103

- 3 videos with 3 different scroll stoppers
- Ad Name - name of your ad
- Upload your creative
- Display Name - brand name
- Text - product name, short benefit, your offer
- CTA - shop now
- URL - product page
- Profile Image - Logo
- Don't need to touch anything else

When To Turn Off Ad Groups

- Turn OFF Ad Group If:
  - If CPC is over $1
  - Spends 0.5x your break-even cost per purchase (BECPP) and no ATC

- If you're ads manager isn't tracking ATCs accurately then disregard this rule
- Spends 1x your BECPP and no sales

*Your break-even cost per purchase (BECPP) = PRODUCT PRICE - PRODUCT COST

NOTE: You ideally want your CPC to be under $0.5, but if you're profitable that's what matters.

Scaling

- Inside of your testing campaign, scale horizontally
  - Duplicate any ad group that makes 3 sales 3 times
- If any of those duplicates make 3 sales as well, duplicate that audience (whether it's broad or interest) 5 times into its own CBO
  - At the time of this video, you can't duplicate ad groups 5 times into a new CBO campaign so I just make a new CBO campaign and use the interest and duplicate it 5 times
  - If the duplicated CBO campaign does well then duplicate (can't actually duplicate I just mean remake) it again and double the budget

- o If you're not comfortable (capital wise) doubling the budget, then just keep it the same
- In parallel to all of this duplicating, continue to test new audiences and new ads inside of your initial testing campaign that you created
- Also, if any of your ad groups do well inside of your testing campaign, keep duplicating them! Don't worry if you get to 50, or even 100 ad groups inside your testing campaign, it's normal
- In my experience, ad groups only last 3-5 days at max, so if yours are dying out, don't be too worried

The Key to Scaling TikTok Ads

- The key to scaling TikTok ads is...CONTINUOUSLY MAKING NEW CREATIVES
- There are 2 ways that you can freshen up your content
  - Making an entirely new video
    - Entirely new concept that is not remotely similar to original vid
  - Creating different iterations of your winning video
    - Change the text to speech
    - Change the music
    - New first clip
  - I've found that changing these aspects of the video has completely refreshed my creative

- What are the 3 main levers that you can pull when split testing new ad creatives
  - SOUNDS
  - TEXT TO SPEECH
  - SCROLL STOPPER

Making Your Own Custom Content

- This is going to separate you from everyone else doing TikTok ads
- The key to making good content, is to understand the platform
- This will help you identify viral trends
- Viral songs will make your content seamlessly fit into the feed
- Order the product off Amazon
- TikTok is raw, organic content
- Add text to speech
- Add tiktok style fonts
- Good example to look at: social_savannah on Twitter
- Billo is a great way to get UGC to embed into your video ads
  - Can be a good way to test some new scroll stoppers

INFLUENCER MARKETING

https://collabstr.com/

CHAPTER ELEVEN

BRANDING TUTORIAL

by Vedank Mohan

Digital Brand Assets

- How to choose your brand name
- How to choose your colours
- Picking your brand identity
- Customer support branding
- Branding your creatives

Physical Brand Assets

- Packaging branding
- Thank you cards
- Bags & Gifts
- Product branding
- Manual branding

Phone welcome message

- Get a phone number online
- Get a royalty free music online
- Hire anyone from Fiverr to do the voice over
- If you have the budget, hire a VA online to answer the phone calls

Branding your creatives

- Hire a content creator (influencer or billo.app)
- Send them a product with a branded box
- Make sure they do a unboxing and mention the brand name
- Put a watermark on your creatives

Physical Brand Assets

- Packaging branding
- Thank you cards

- Bags & Gifts
- Product branding
- Manual branding

Packaging branding

- Ask your agent for the package dimensions
- Hire a designer from Fiverr
- Make sure the design is clean & classy
- If low budget: go to a local printing store
- If enough volume: ask to your agent to include the branded box in the pricing
- Make sure the carton quality is decent. Do NOT try to save on this!

114

Useful links

- Brand Name Generator: www.namelix.com
- Color scheme: www.coolors.co

CHAPTER TWELVE

VIRTUAL ASSISTANTS

(FIND, HIRE & TRAIN VAs)

by Mohamed Nazar Mahmoud

When should you hire a Virtual Assistant

1. Consistent Sales

Min. 5-10 Orders per Day

2. Profitability

Your Profit Margin is enough to generate you an Extra Income

3. Ready to Scale Your Business

You want to spend your time learning about scaling and growing your business instead of having time consuming tasks that won't help you move forward.

4. Acquire Know-How

You feel like there are some skills missing in your Business like negotiating with suppliers, better customer support or better graphics for your store.

5. Work-Life-Balance getting out of hand

You're spending more time in front of your screen than with your Friends & Family. You have to free up some time.

What A Virtual Assistant can do for you

1. Order Fulfillment

The VA makes sure that your orders get fulfilled every day and tracking numbers sent to the customers

2. Customer Support

The VA will answer all your Emails, DMs & Comments on Social Media Platforms or Live Chat questions coming from customers

3. Store Management

The VA can create a Store for you, do the Product Research, Manage Paypal & Stripe Cases, Stay in Touch with the Supplier, Setup Social Media Pages and Run Ads

4. Random Tasks

You can ask a VA for any task you feel he's qualified to do it (e.g. managing finances)

Where to hire a Virtual Assistant

1. Upwork

2. Fiverr

3. Monazar Marketing

Costs of Hiring a Virtual Assistants

Average Costs per month: $300-500 for Order Fulfillment & Customer Support

Choosing the Right Candidate

1. Add Task to Listing

Add a Question like «What's 2+2?» to the listing to see if the applicants actually read the listing

2. Experience & Availability

Check for Skills & Experiences of the applicants. Shopify or Customer Support is preferred. How much time can they invest? How good is their English? Check previous reviews or their portfolio if provided.

3. Soft Skills

Communication, Trust, Loyalty, Likeability and General Intelligence

How To Train your Virtual Assistants

1. Be There for Them in the Beginning

Invest your time in the beginning to show your Virtual Assistants exactly what you expect. Low expectations in the first Week.

2. **Be Approachable and Open for Questions**

Create an environment where your VAs know that they can ask you questions whenever needed. Discuss all the DO's and DONT's for Your Business (e.g. what Authorities they have, letting them know what important policies you are following)

3. **Control the Work**

Set Deadlines, check the Work done & give Feedback. Discuss How the Reporting should be (Daily, Weekly or Monthly).

Where to Be Careful

1. Credit Card Details

Use Debit Cards, Follow Transactions in the Beginning

2. Logins

Create New Passwords, Add them as Staff Member (Shopify, Limited Permissions)

3. Follow The Work Done

Check if Emails are correctly replied to, Orders Fulfilled in the right way and consistently (Double Check Numbers).

Monazar Marketing Virtual Assistants

Benefits - www.monazar.com/vas

1. Shopify-Trained, Reliable Virtual Assistants

2. Easy Payment

3. Having Mohamed as a Contact Person for questions and

uncertainties

4. 7-Day Money Back Guarantee

5. Free Customer Support Template

How to Get Organized – Tools to Use

1. Trello

Helps with Managing Tasks and Projects

2. Whatsapp / Telegram

Use for Daily Communication

CHAPTER THIRTEEN

Tiktok/Instagram Organic

Find A TIK TOK Organic Winning Product Step By Step

Step 1: Search Tiktok Made Me Buy It and filter the videos to the most popular/most engaged of the week. You want to do this, to weed out all of the saturated and old products.

Step 2: Click on all the top video products that you notice and see how many views they are getting, monitor their engagement levels, see if they have a functioning store, and see if they are still uploading consistently and frequently. (you want to do this, because, if they are still posting and have positive engagement, odds are they are generating sales.

Step 3: You want to search for videos preferably that have hit over 1 million views and under 10 million because that leaves plenty of room for you to come in. videos with hundreds of thousands are also a sweet spot.

Step 4: Search for the product niche hashtag on tiktok to see how many views that niche is getting and if it is popular.

Step 5: you want to make sure the niche is getting tens if not hundreds of millions of views on multiple videos

Step 6: Search for the product on Aliexpress and began promoting once the profit margins align, profit margins must be above 40%

How to create organic content that will go viral

Step 1: Replicate your competitor's most viral video

Step 2: Introduce trending sounds and hashtags to your content

Step 3: Camera quality must be decent, Use Tiktoks Enhancing Effect To Make Your Video Appear Higher Quality

Step 4: remake sounds and focuses on creating good satisfying sounds

Step 5: Keep your videos at a good pace

Step 6: Edit your videos on tiktok, tiktok pushes out videos edited on their platform.

BONUS

Tiktok is pushing longer videos 15-45 seconds

Horizontal videos are going to become a thing, make sure to implement some of those.

Mistakes to avoid on TikTok Organic

- Avoid engaging with your account
- Avoid stealing other people's content
- Avoid buying followers
- Avoid being inconsistent
- How To Analyze Your Content/Account
- Your account should be growing
- Views should be at least over 200 in the first 48 hours.
- Your followers should be growing
- Like the view, the ratio should be no higher than a 1/50

Your comments should be positive It takes 2 weeks, sometimes more of uploading every day to really hit the algorithm and go viral. It takes time. Always be consistent and keep testing products out.